HOW OUR BODIES WORK

BIRTH and GROWTH

JAN BURGESS

Editorial planning
Philip Steele

M
MACMILLAN

First published 1989
Reprinted 1989

Published by
MACMILLAN EDUCATION LTD
Houndmills, Basingstoke, Hampshire RG21 2XS
and London
Companies and representatives
throughout the world

Designed and produced by BLA Publishing Limited,
East Grinstead, Sussex, England.

Also in LONDON · HONG KONG · TAIPEI · SINGAPORE · NEW YORK

A Ling Kee Company

Illustrations by David Anstey; Sallie Alane Reason; Val Sangster/Linden Artists and Linda Thursby/Linden Artists
Printed in Hong Kong

British Library Cataloguing in Publication Data

Burgess, Jan
  Birth and growth. — (How our bodies work)
  — (Macmillan world library)
  1. Human growth — Juvenile literature
  I. Title   II. Steele, Philip   III. Series
  612.6   QP84

ISBN 0–333–45967–9

Photographic credits

t = top b = bottom l = left r = right

cover: Trevor Hill

4 S. & R. Greenhill; 5*t*, 5*b* Frank Lane Picture Agency; 6 ZEFA; 11, 13 Science Photo Library; 15*t* Trevor Hill; 15*b*, 16 S. & R. Greenhill; 17 Rex Features; 18 Camilla Jessel; 19 Science Photo Library; 20 ZEFA; 21, 22*t*, 22*b*, 23, 24, 25*t* Trevor Hill; 25*b*, 26, 27*t* Camilla Jessel; 27*b*, 28, 29*t* Trevor Hill; 29*b* S. & R. Greenhill; 30, 31, 32, 33*t* Trevor Hill; 33*b* 34*t*, 34*b* S. & R. Greenhill; 35 Camilla Jessel; 36 Rex Features; 37*t* The Hutchison Library; 37*b* Rex Features; 38, 39*t* Trevor Hill; 39*b*, 40*t* S. & R. Greenhill; 40*b* Rex Features; 41 Trevor Hill; 42, 43*t*, 43*b* The Hutchison Library

Note to the reader
In this book there are some words in the text which are printed in **bold** type. This shows that the word is listed in the glossary on page 46. The glossary gives a brief explanation of words which may be new to you.

Contents

Introduction

The story of how a baby is born and how it grows up is one of the most amazing that there is. Many animals take only a few weeks or months to become adults. Human babies take much longer.

It is about 20 years from the time a human baby is born until it becomes an adult and stops growing. And all this time, the young human is learning new things about the world around him or her.

Animals and eggs

All animals, including humans, eventually get old and die. New young animals grow up to take their place. This is vital if each kind of animal, or **species**, is to grow and survive. The way creatures make new copies of themselves is called **reproduction**.

One species reproduces in a different way from another. Simple animals, such as an amoeba, just divide in half. An amoeba has no fixed shape and lives in water. When it divides, each half swims away, a complete amoeba. The problem with this kind of reproduction is that it does not allow for any change in the animal. The children are exactly the same as the parent, that is they are **identical**.

More complex animals have two different kinds or **sexes**, a male and a female. A tiny part of the male, called a **sperm**, joins up with a tiny part of the female, called an egg. This process is called **fertilization**. The new young creature that grows from the fertilized egg has some features of the male and some of the female. It is not exactly the same as either of its parents. This is called **sexual reproduction**.

▼ Human babies take many years to grow into adults. They must be cared for by their parents and other members of the family.

▼ Frogspawn floats in a pond. The female common frog lays about 2000 eggs in just a few seconds. The male fertilizes them straight after they have been laid.

Giving birth

Sometimes the fertilized egg grows inside the mother's body. Sometimes it grows outside. Birds, fish and many reptiles lay their eggs. The baby grows in the egg until it is ready to hatch. Fish and many reptiles can look after themselves as soon as they hatch. Baby birds have to be fed and kept warm in the nest.

The fertilized egg of many animals grows inside its mother's body. This includes the egg of a human being. The egg is kept safe and warm in the mother's body. When the baby is born, it cannot survive on its own. It needs milk from its mother's body. It has to be kept safe from danger while it grows and learns to take care of itself.

▼ A foal can stand and run almost as soon as it is born. Like human babies, it feeds on its mother's milk.

Female and male

▼ For the first few years boys and girls have a similar body shape. As they grow into adults their bodies change so that it is easy to see the differences between men and women.

The male and female kinds of every species are slightly different. They have different parts, or **organs**, which are made just for reproduction. The body of the human male produces sperm. The sperm fertilizes the female egg, and the egg begins to grow into a baby. The body of the human female is made so that a baby can grow inside her.

Men's bodies

Men's bodies are larger and firmer than women's. Between their legs, men have an organ called a **penis**. The sperm leaves a man's body through his penis. Behind the penis is a bag of skin called the **scrotum**.

Inside the scrotum millions of sperm are made. They are made and stored in two **testes** inside the scrotum. The sperm travel from each testis to the penis along a tube called the **vas deferens**.

Sperm are too small to see with the naked eye. Millions and millions of them are made, but each female egg can only be fertilized by one sperm.

Women's bodies

Women are usually slightly smaller than men. Their bodies are softer and more rounded. Inside a woman's body are all the parts needed for a baby to grow. She has two small **ovaries** where the eggs are made.

The female egg is called an **ovum**. When there are more than one, they are known as ova. The human ovum is tiny. It is smaller than a pinhead.

When an ovum is ready, it travels out of the ovary down one of two **fallopian tubes**. The fallopian tubes lead to a pear-shaped organ called the **uterus**.

If an ovum is fertilized, it grows into a baby inside the uterus. When the baby is ready to be born, it comes into the world through an opening between the mother's legs. This opening is called the **vagina**.

Young babies cannot eat the same food as a child or adult. Their bodies cannot digest the kind of food we eat. Babies suck milk from their mothers' bodies. The milk is made in glands in the mothers' breasts. Babies do not usually need any other food to begin with. Breast milk is the perfect food for several months.

The female reproductive system

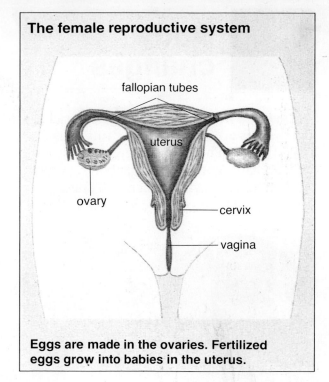

fallopian tubes

uterus

ovary

cervix

vagina

Eggs are made in the ovaries. Fertilized eggs grow into babies in the uterus.

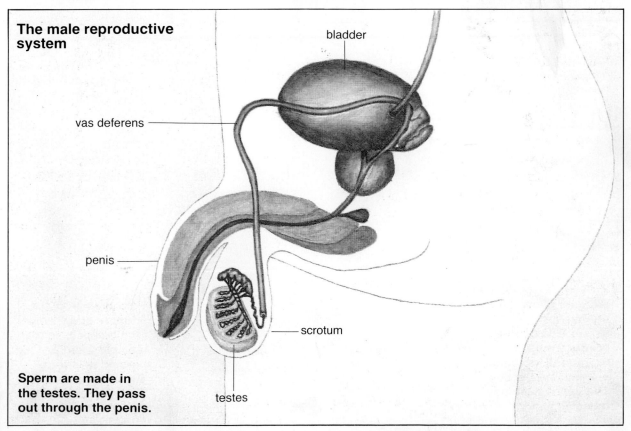

The male reproductive system

bladder

vas deferens

penis

scrotum

testes

Sperm are made in the testes. They pass out through the penis.

7

Body changes

Just as a house is built of many bricks, our bodies are made of many tiny parts called **cells**. There are different kinds of cells in different parts of the body. A new human starts to grow when two special cells join. Those cells are a sperm cell from the father and an ovum from the mother.

The sperm and the ovum merge together. Then they start to divide, like the amoeba, but they do not separate. The cells go on dividing and growing. They make up the millions of cells in the human body.

When humans are young, they cannot have babies or make sperm. It is only as they grow into adults that their bodies change. There are substances in the body which cause these changes. They are called **hormones**. Hormones are made in **glands**.

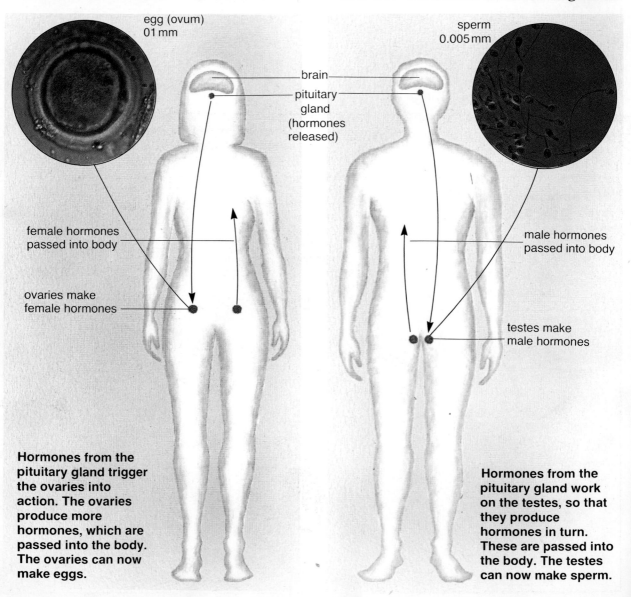

egg (ovum)
01 mm

sperm
0.005 mm

brain

pituitary gland (hormones released)

female hormones passed into body

ovaries make female hormones

male hormones passed into body

testes make male hormones

Hormones from the pituitary gland trigger the ovaries into action. The ovaries produce more hormones, which are passed into the body. The ovaries can now make eggs.

Hormones from the pituitary gland work on the testes, so that they produce hormones in turn. These are passed into the body. The testes can now make sperm.

The hormones pour into the bloodstream and are carried round the body. They control many kinds of activity in our bodies. These include growth, sleep and even how quickly we use up the food we eat.

There are also hormones that cause the male to make sperm and the female to produce ova. These hormones are called sex hormones.

▼ The hormone-producing glands cluster around the blood vessel. The hormones pass through the wall of the blood vessel into the bloodstream.

Hormones in children

We all have sex hormones but in children the amount in their bodies is small. As children get older the levels of sex hormones increase. The sex hormones have different effects in men and women.

In boys, the hormones make the testes grow larger. They start to produce their own male sex hormones. As a result, sperm grow in the testes. In girls, the ovaries get larger and produce their own female sex hormones. Since before birth, many tiny eggs have been stored away in the ovaries. Now they start to ripen. From time to time, a ripe ovum bursts out of one of the ovaries. If it meets up with a male sperm, a new baby will begin to grow.

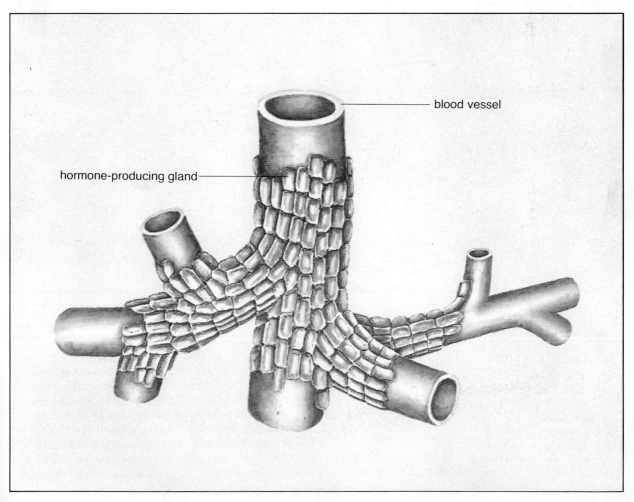

blood vessel

hormone-producing gland

Creating life

A woman's body has to go through many changes to get it ready for a new baby to develop. Every 28 days or so, hormones cause a ripe ovum to be swept out of one of the ovaries. The ovum moves gently along the fallopian tube until it reaches the uterus. If the ovum has not been fertilized by a sperm, it dies within two days.

The uterus has a special lining. This softens and fills with blood ready to receive the fertilized ovum. When the ovum dies, the lining is shed from the woman's body through the vagina. This shedding of the uterus lining is called **menstruation**. It happens every month and usually lasts 4 or 5 days. Then the whole pattern starts again. Another tiny ovum journeys down the fallopian tube.

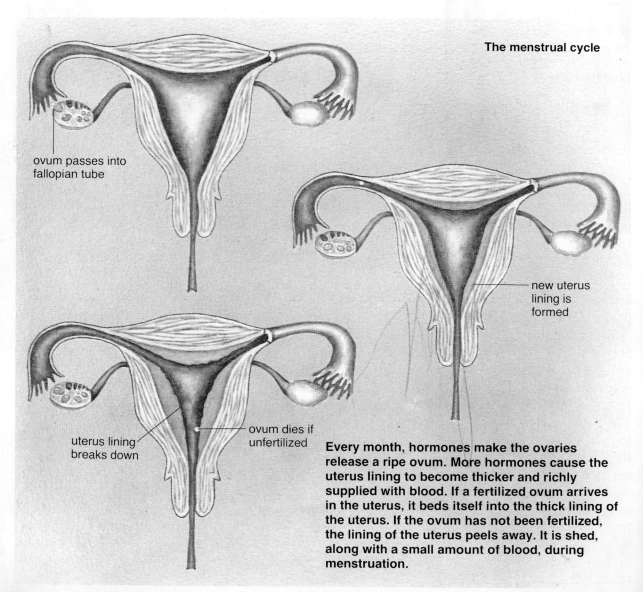

The menstrual cycle

ovum passes into fallopian tube

new uterus lining is formed

uterus lining breaks down

ovum dies if unfertilized

Every month, hormones make the ovaries release a ripe ovum. More hormones cause the uterus lining to become thicker and richly supplied with blood. If a fertilized ovum arrives in the uterus, it beds itself into the thick lining of the uterus. If the ovum has not been fertilized, the lining of the uterus peels away. It is shed, along with a small amount of blood, during menstruation.

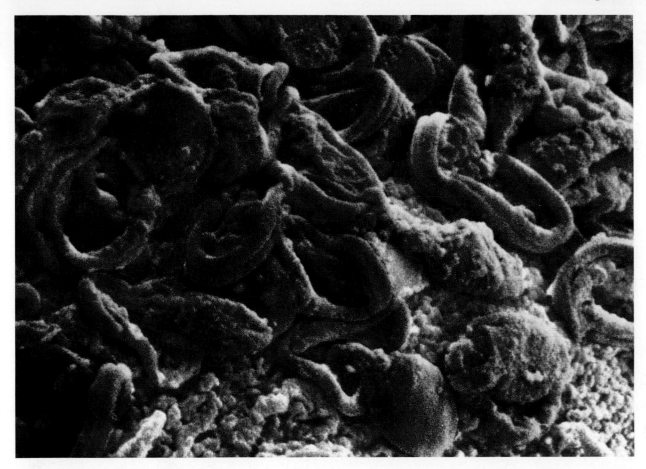

Joining together

To fertilize an ovum, a sperm has to get inside the woman's body. The sperm leaves the man's penis in a sticky white liquid called **semen**. Semen protects the sperm. Semen will not come out of the penis unless the penis has become hard. When a man and woman wish to join together, the woman's vagina becomes soft and slippery. The man can slide his penis inside her vagina. The semen will then rush out of the penis. This coming together of a man and woman is called **sexual intercourse**.

The semen contains hundreds of millions of sperm, but only one of them will join up with an ovum. The sperm have lashing tails that help them swim. They swim up into the uterus. Only a couple a thousand reach the openings into the fallopian tubes.

▲ This picture has been magnified many times. It shows human sperm trying to burrow into an egg, or ovum. Sperms produce a chemical which helps them pass through the outer layer of the egg and fertilize it.

The sperm swim into the tubes, searching for an ovum. When they find it, they surround it and try to burrow into it. Finally, one sperm manages to get inside the ovum and fertilizes it. A new life begins. The moment that the sperm is inside the ovum, the ovum changes and no other sperms can enter it.

Within a short time, the fertilized ovum divides into two cells, then four, then eight cells. This is the start of many cell divisions as a new baby begins to form.

In the uterus

The fertilized ovum continues to move along the fallopian tube. It takes about a week to travel from the ovary to the uterus. When the ovum reaches the uterus, it burrows into the lining. The lining has thickened ready to receive it. The lining has a very good supply of blood. This blood provides food and oxygen for the growing group of cells.

Taking shape

A mother with a baby growing inside her is said to be **pregnant**. She knows that she may be pregnant when she does not see the usual signs of menstruation. An ovum has been fertilized, so the lining of the uterus has not been shed.

By the time the mother has been pregnant for just seven weeks, the baby, or **foetus**, is less than 1.5 cm long. However, many parts of the foetus are already recognizable as a baby. The heart is already beating, and tiny arms and legs are starting to grow. By 14 weeks the foetus is properly formed. It is still only about 7.5 cm long. It still has a lot of growing to do. The foetus could not yet survive on its own outside its mother's body.

There is still plenty of room for the foetus to move around. The mother may feel it moving at about 16-20 weeks. At about 16 weeks, the mother's stomach starts to get larger to make room for the growing foetus. At the end of pregnancy, her uterus has stretched to many times its normal size.

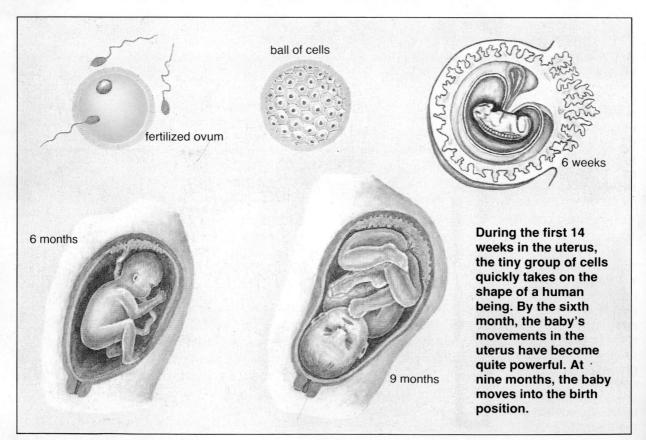

ball of cells

fertilized ovum

6 weeks

6 months

9 months

During the first 14 weeks in the uterus, the tiny group of cells quickly takes on the shape of a human being. By the sixth month, the baby's movements in the uterus have become quite powerful. At nine months, the baby moves into the birth position.

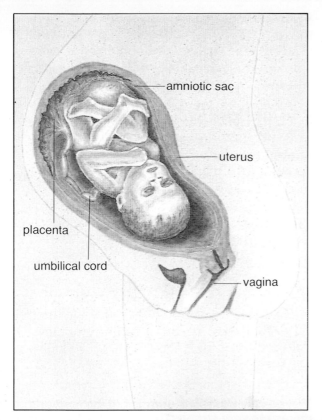

amniotic sac

uterus

placenta

umbilical cord

vagina

Life support system

All the time the foetus is inside its mother, it is surrounded by a kind of bag. The bag is full of liquid called **amniotic fluid**. The foetus floats around inside the bag, or **amniotic sac**, protected by its mother's body.

Even before it is born the foetus needs food. The foetus gets the food from **nutrients**. These are tiny particles found in the mother's blood. A tube called the **umbilical cord** links the foetus to its mother. The umbilical cord is the foetus's lifeline. It leads to an organ called the **placenta**. In the placenta, the foetus's blood comes very close to the mother's blood, although they do not actually mix. Nutrients and oxygen pass from the mother's blood to the foetus's. Wastes from the foetus go across to the placenta and into the mother's bloodstream to be washed away. Your tummy button is the place where your umbilical cord once grew.

▲ The baby is curled up snugly in the uterus, protected by the fluid of the amniotic sac. The umbilical cord links the baby to the placenta, which acts as a life-support system.

► This baby has just been born. The umbilical cord is still attached to her stomach. Her skin is protected by a white greasy substance called vernix. Soon she will open her eyes to see the world for the first time.

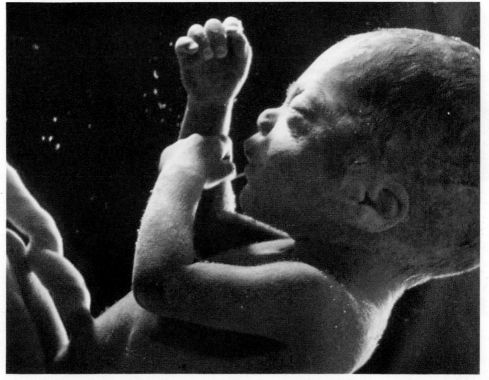

13

Giving birth

After about 40 weeks inside its mother's body, the new baby is ready to come out into the world. By this time, there is not much room for it to move about. Most babies have turned upside-down, as they are usually born head first.

The **muscles** in our body make it possible for us to move. The uterus is made up of very strong muscles. When a baby is ready to be born, hormones start off movements in these muscles. These movements are called **contractions**. The muscles tighten for a minute or two and then relax.

First of all, this tightening of the muscle makes the opening of the uterus get larger. This opening is called the **cervix**. The cervix needs to be wide enough for the baby to squeeze through. This may take several hours and can be quite painful for the mother as these muscles have not been used before. Before a baby is born, the amniotic sac surrounding the baby breaks, and the liquid inside pours out.

Into the world

When the cervix is fully open, or **dilated**, the baby's head can squeeze through into the vagina. More contractions push the baby out into the world. The baby takes its first breath on its own. It is time for the mother and father to see whether they have a boy or a girl. The mother can also have a rest after the hard work of giving birth.

Soon after the baby has been born, the umbilical cord is cut. This is quite painless for mother and baby. The placenta, which has now done all its work, is also pushed out through the vagina.

▼ A baby is born. The muscles of the mother's uterus are very strong. They push the baby into the world head-first.

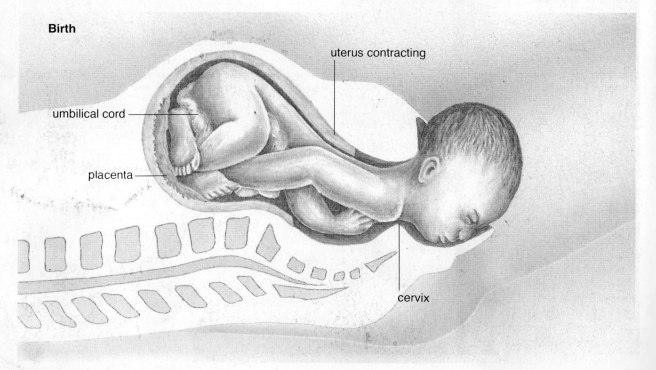

Birth

umbilical cord

placenta

uterus contracting

cervix

▶ Sometimes babies like this are born too soon. Their bodies cannot keep warm so they are often put in an incubator. The incubator is a special box which keeps the babies warm and protects them from germs.

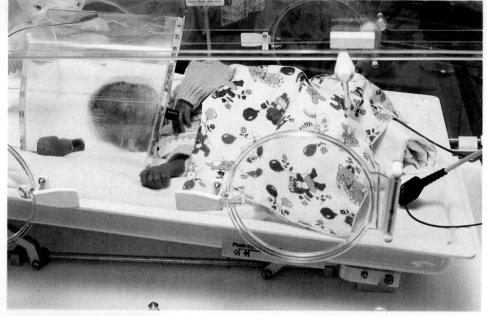

▼ The birth may take several hours. It is very hard work! At last the baby is born and the mother can rest. These proud parents are delighted with their new baby.

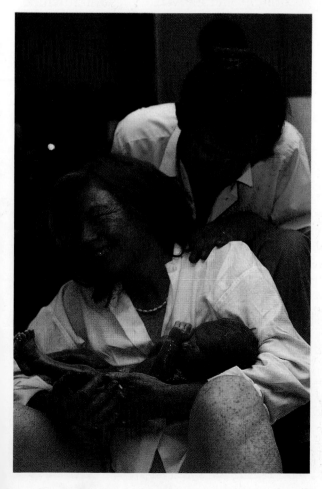

Home or hospital

For some women, home is the best place to have a baby. They feel safe and secure in their own familiar surroundings, with someone to help them. However, in many countries, most babies are born in hospital. Both at home and in hospital, there are specially trained nurses to help the mother and her baby during the birth. These nurses are called **midwives**.

In hospital, there is special equipment to keep checks on the baby or to help if the baby has trouble breathing. This has made childbirth safer for many mothers and their babies.

In many parts of the world, women have to give birth far away from well-equipped hospitals. Childbirth is still dangerous. Mothers sometimes die from losing too much blood. Also, babies may be damaged if the birth takes too long.

Some fathers want to be with their partners when their baby is born. Most parents look back on the births of their children as exciting and dramatic events. For the child, it was the most important birthday of his or her life!

Twins

Usually a mother has only one baby at a time. However, some women give birth to two babies, or twins.

Looking alike

Twins that look exactly alike are called **identical twins**. Right at the beginning of pregnancy, the fertilized ovum splits into two. Each half then grows into a separate complete baby. Each twin has its own amniotic sac, but they share just one placenta. While they are growing inside their mother, their bloodstreams actually mix in the placenta.

▼ Identical twins are always both either boys or girls. They grew from the same ovum and sperm so they are often very difficult to tell apart.

Because they grew from the same ovum and sperm, both babies are either boys or girls. They have the same hair and eye colour. As they grow up they often become very close to each other. To anyone outside the family, it may be very hard to tell one from the other.

Looking different

Normally, just one ovum is released from one of the ovaries at a time. Sometimes more than one ovum is released. If two ova are fertilized by two sperm, then both the ova will grow into babies at the same time.

The mother will give birth to twins, but they will not be identical. Each grew from a different ovum and sperm. They have separate placentae. They may be different sexes and may have quite different colouring. They are just like normal brothers and sisters except that they were born at the same time. These twins are called **fraternal twins**.

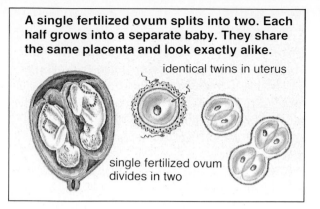

A single fertilized ovum splits into two. Each half grows into a separate baby. They share the same placenta and look exactly alike.

identical twins in uterus

single fertilized ovum divides in two

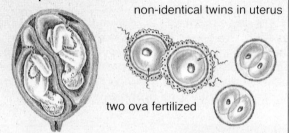

The ovary releases two ova at once. If both are fertilized, two babies grow in the uterus at once. They have separate placentae and may look quite different.

non-identical twins in uterus

two ova fertilized

More than two

Sometimes two, three or even more ova may be released. If all the ova are fertilized, then several babies will grow at once. The mother is said to have a **multiple birth**. Four babies are called quadruplets or quads, five babies are quintuplets or quins. Six babies are called sextuplets, but they are very rare. Humans do not often give birth to more than two babies at once.

A woman may want to have a baby, but finds that she does not become pregnant. Doctors can give her drugs that help the ovaries to release their ova. The drugs may work too well. This is often the cause of a multiple birth.

▼ These children are quins. All five were born at the same time. Because some are boys and some are girls and they do not look exactly alike, we know that several ova were fertilized at the same time.

The body programme

While a mother is waiting for her baby to be born, she will probably wonder what it will look like. Will it be a boy or a girl? Will it have brown eyes or blue?

Just as a computer has a program to tell it what to do, so our bodies have a programme to tell each part how to grow. This body programme, or pattern, contains instructions for every detail about us, from the colour of our hair to the shape of our little toes. It takes the form of a chemical message which is passed on from parents to children at the moment when the sperm fertilizes the ovum. The code is stored away in tiny thread-like structures which are called **chromosomes**.

New cells

Each cell in your body has 46 chromosomes, which are arranged in pairs. However, the sperm and ovum have only 23 chromosomes each. At the moment of fertilization, the 23 chromosomes from the mother's cell pair up with the 23 chromosomes from the father's. This makes the full total of 46.

When the fertilized egg divides into two, a copy of the 46 chromosomes is made for the new cell. Eventually, every one of the millions and millions of cells in your body will contain a copy of the original 46 chromosomes. This makes up your body pattern.

▼ **The ovum contains 23 chromosomes from the mother. The sperm has 23 chromosomes from the father in its head. This new baby has half her chromosomes from her mother and half from her father. This will make her look rather like both of her parents when she grows up.**

▲ Sperm carry either an X or a Y chromosome. If an X chromosome from the father joins with an X chromosome from the mother, the baby will be a girl. If a Y chromosome joins with the X from the mother, the baby will be a boy.

▼ These greatly magnified chromsomes from one cell are grouped in 23 pairs. The last pair are not matched. They are an X and a Y chromosome. This shows the cell comes from a boy.

Boy or girl?

Your 46 chromosomes are like steps in a knitting pattern. Each step contains the instructions for a different part of you. The ovum and sperm cells contain just one chromosome each which give the instructions for making a boy or a girl. These are the sex chromosomes.

The sex chromosome in the ovum is always called an X chromosome. The sex chromosome carried by the sperm can be either an X or a Y chromosome. If an X chromosome from the father joins the X chromosome from the mother, the developing baby will be a girl. If the sperm carries a Y chromosome, it will be a boy.

It is pure chance whether the fertilizing sperm carries an X or a Y chromosome. If doctors could separate out the X and Y carrying sperm, parents may be able to choose whether to have a boy or a girl.

From parents to child

There are nearly 500 million people in the world, yet every human being is unlike any other. This is because we each have our own set of chromosomes to make up our own body pattern. This body pattern is different from anyone else's.

Chromosomes are made of strings of separate blocks called **genes**. Genes are like packets of information or instructions. How tall we grow, whether we will be star footballers or guitarists depends largely on the genes with which we are born.

Family likenesses

Your genes were passed on to you from your parents. Half come from your mother and half from your father. This is why members of families often look like each other. The genes that gave grandmother curly hair may have been passed on to your mother, and then in turn to you.

The way genes are passed on from one generation to the next is called **heredity**. The study of genes and how they work is called **genetics**.

▼ Three generations line up for a family photograph. Can you see any family likenesses? Does the girl look like her mother? Does the boy look like his father and his grandmother?

Heredity or surroundings?

Brothers and sisters may grow up to look quite similar to each other, but be quite different in character. Or they may look very different, but be alike in character. Usually, brothers and sisters have half their genes alike.

Some of the things people inherit in their genes cannot be changed. Others are affected by what happens around them and their surroundings, or **environment**. For example, your genes might mean that you enjoy music. However, if you do not have the chance to learn the piano, you are unlikely to become a great pianist.

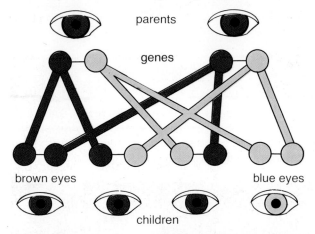

parents

genes

brown eyes
blue eyes

children

There are several types of skin and many eye colours. Your skin type and the colour of your eyes are laid down in your genes and cannot be altered. Some genes are stronger than others. For example, the gene for brown eyes is stronger than for blue eyes. If both parents have blue eyes, their children will almost certainly have blue eyes too. However, if both parents have brown eyes, there is still a small chance that they will have blue-eyed children. This happens if one of the grandparents or great-grandparents had blue eyes. If one parent has blue eyes, and one has brown, their children are more likely to have brown eyes.

Survival kit

A newborn baby has not yet had time to learn about the world in which he finds himself. However, a new baby will suck milk without learning how to do it. He or she will also cry loudly when hungry, until food is provided. Both these kinds of behaviour make sure that the baby gets the food he needs to survive and grow. They are examples of **instinct**. Instincts are passed on to us in our genes.

▲ What colour are your eyes? Are they the same colour as your parents' or your grandparents'? Eye colour depends on genes passed on from one generation to the next.

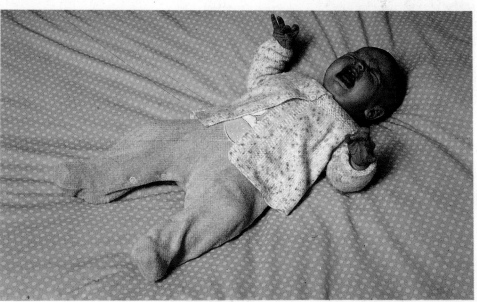

▶ Babies cannot talk, but they can certainly yell! They do this to let us know that they need attention. They might be tired, hungry or in pain.

Newborn babies

The moment of birth is a time of great change for babies. For nine months they have been curled up in the warmth and safety of their mothers' bodies. A steady supply of food and oxygen has been piped in through the umbilical cord. Their mothers' bodies have done all the work of breathing and taking in food for them.

Within a few seconds of arriving in the world, they have to take their first gulp of air. Their lungs fill and start working on their own. Very soon after birth, their mothers' blood supply to the umbilical cord shuts down. Once the cord has been cut, the babies are on their own.

▲ A baby sleeps in his mother's arms. Babies become used to the rocking and swaying of the mother's body when they are in the uterus. A newborn baby sleeps much longer than an adult.

▼ Young babies get their food from milk. As they grow older they need to have different foods. At first the food usually has to be made smooth and quite runny as babies cannot chew.

► Young babies stare at human faces. They soon learn to tell their parents' faces from the others. From about six weeks old babies can smile at their parents.

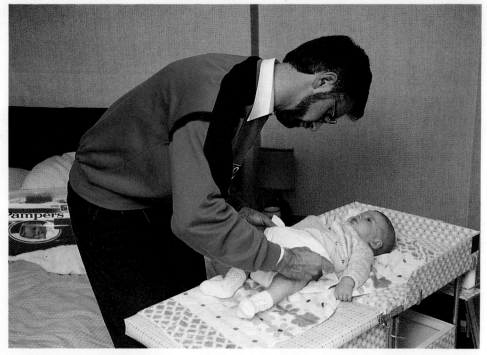

Programmed to survive

At birth, babies do not know anything about the world in which they find themselves. They cannot move about or even feed themselves. However, they are not as helpless as they look. They can suck milk strongly. They can cry loudly when they are cold, hungry or uncomfortable. In a very short time, they learn to recognize and respond to the person who is caring for them.

Food

Babies have to adjust to a new way of feeding as well as a new way of breathing. For the nine months before birth, food has been supplied in a ready-to-use form, straight from the mother's blood supply. After birth the best food for babies continues to come from their mothers as milk from their breasts.

Milk is made by hormones which work on glands in the mothers' breasts. The milk contains the right complex mix of nutrients that the baby needs. For the first few days, the early milk or **colostrum** is full of extra nutrients.

The baby nuzzles against the breast and fastens onto the tip of the breast, or nipple. The baby can then suck out the breast milk. The more the baby sucks, the more the glands in the breast make milk to keep him or her satisfied.

Babies need to be fed very often in the first few weeks after the birth. It is a few months before their teeth begin to grow and babies learn to chew solid food.

Babies and illness

Our bodies have to learn how to fight off disease. Our blood supply learns to recognize **germs** that invade the body. To fight these germs, the blood makes **antibodies**. These antibodies stay in the blood and defend us against the germs the next time they strike.

The antibodies in the mother's blood protect the growing foetus in the uterus. The antibodies in her breast milk help to protect the young baby against disease.

Learning to move

▼ Most babies go through a similar pattern of development. They have to gain control of the muscles in their backs before they can sit, crawl or walk. Some babies never learn to crawl. They go straight from sitting on the floor to standing and walking.

During pregnancy, babies lie curled up in the uterus. At birth, they unfold and stretch out their legs and back for the first time. Their bony framework, or **skeleton**, is fully formed. At this stage, however, much of it is made of a tough tissue called **cartilage**. Cartilage is softer than bone, but over the next few years it will gradually harden.

An adult has 206 separate bones. A baby has about 350. In time, some of the baby's bones will grow together. For example, a baby's skull is made of separate plates. This allows the head to 'give' a little as it is squeezed down through the mother's vagina at birth. During the first few years, the plates grow together. They form a rigid box which protects the brain.

Moving about

Like children and adults, every baby is different from every other. Some cry a lot. Some do not. Some begin to grow teeth at six months. Some do not start until they are a year old. However, as babies grow, one change usually follows after another in the same set order.

At birth, babies have little control over their muscles. They can move their arms and legs, and turn their heads. However, they cannot sit, roll over or even lift up their heads. Over the next few weeks, babies gradually get control over the muscles in their necks. By about six weeks, a baby can hold its head up for just a second or two. A few days later, he or she can hold it up long enough to look round.

Gradually, the baby develops muscle control elsewhere in the body. When a baby is first sat on the floor, he or she will probably roll forward, back sagging. Not until six or seven months of age can most babies sit with a straight back. Then, one day, they will try to reach out for a toy. They will find themselves rolling forward onto their hands and knees. Soon they take their first crawling step.

The more babies use their muscles, the stronger they get. Before they are a year old, many babies are trying to pull themselves up on to their feet. By instinct, they reach out for help from anyone who will help them. Even a piece of furniture will do.

▼ Many babies will practise walking for hours. They often fall over. They must learn to balance, just as a circus clown learns to balance on a tightrope.

▼ In many countries, clinics are held so that doctors and other health advisors can keep a check on babies. This helps to keep babies healthy.

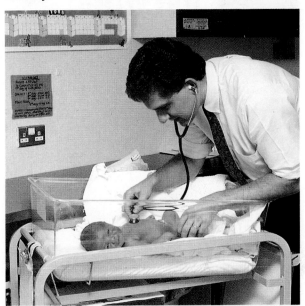

Aware of the world

As soon as a baby comes into the world, he is surrounded by things to feel, hear, see, taste and smell. All these things are called **stimuli**. From that first moment, a baby has to start sorting out and making sense of the flood of stimuli.

We do not know exactly how newborn babies sense the world. They cannot tell us what they see or hear. However, the way they behave gives us many clues.

The senses

We know babies can feel. They like to be cuddled and held firmly. This will calm and soothe a fretful baby. We know they can hear clearly, because they jump if startled by a sudden noise. They also respond to the sounds of voices by turning their heads to listen. They can do this from the first three or four days after they are born. If they are crying they may be soothed by a recording of a heartbeat. This is the sound they have been listening to in the uterus throughout the nine months of pregnancy.

We know that at first babies are **short-sighted**. This means that they only see clearly over a distance of 20 to 25 centimetres. Beyond this range things look blurred. Babies will tend to look at a light patch across the room, such as a bright window. They respond better to things held close to them, especially the human face. Babies seem to learn and recognize the faces of the people looking after them from very early on.

◄ This baby is studying his grandfather's face very closely. He is using his eyes and ears to try to make sense of what he is seeing and hearing.

▼ As children grow up they may be checked to make sure they can hear properly. This child should turn in the direction of the rattle if her hearing is alright.

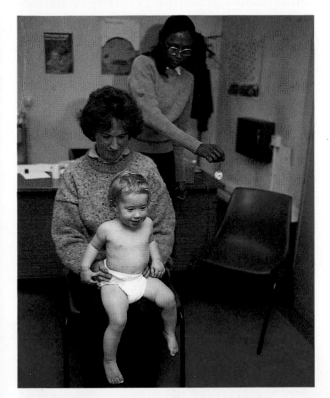

The flavour of food and drink is picked up by structures called **taste buds**. In adults, these taste buds are found mostly on the tongue, and there are some elsewhere in the mouth and in the throat. Babies have many more taste buds than an adult. Also their taste buds are found everywhere inside the mouth.

The first year

Babies learn about the world around them by using all their senses. They pick up toys, look at them, touch them, and then bite and chew them. Bit by bit, they learn what is likely to be good to eat, or when something will be painful because it is prickly, or too hot or too cold.

At the same time, their senses develop so that they can respond in more ways to different stimuli. They also begin to make sense of the babble of language that they have been hearing since birth.

▼ This child is concentrating on his toy. His senses are telling him about its colour, shape and whether it is hard or soft.

Speech

The ability to speak to each other is what makes human beings different from every other animal. By using language in the form of speech, reading and writing, we can exchange complex ideas, and store them for our children and their children in the years to come.

First words

A small baby gets across his or her basic needs without needing speech. Most mothers can tell if their babies are tired, hungry or in pain by the differences in the tone or strength of their cries.

In the first few months, as well as crying, babies make gentle cooing noises. As the baby gets older, the noises become more varied. Babies do not just copy sounds like talking parrots. Babies learn language by hearing it being used. They understand a great deal before they start to talk themselves.

Towards the end of the first year, many babies say their first words. These are likely to be labels for things that give them pleasure, such as people, animals or favourite things. 'Mummy', 'dog' or 'biscuit' are good examples. In their second year they usually learn to add new words on to those labels. Now they might say 'more biccit' or 'where teddy'. In the second and third year, there is a great advance in language. Children begin to put together words to make sentences. By the age of five, they are using 1200 to 2000 words. Some adults know 25 000 words or more.

▼ Small babies make a stream of sounds. This gradually turns into single words. Simple speech is often helped along by pointing.

▼ Children who cannot hear properly often have trouble pronouncing difficult sounds. This speech therapist is teaching this child the difference in sound between the words 'pan' and 'fan'.

Speech problems

Some children have problems learning to speak. The most serious speech problems are caused by deafness. Babies born deaf cry normally. For the first few months, they make the same babbling noises as normal babies. Soon the babbling dies down. It does not develop into speech because a deaf baby cannot hear the language around him. For deaf children, learning to communicate is a slow and painful process. Trained workers called speech therapists can help.

▼ Very deaf children often cannot speak clearly at all. They cannot hear what the words should sound like. They are taught sign language so they can 'speak' using their hands. Each letter and some common words have special signs.

Using your brain

▼ Children have a built-in curiosity about the world around them. Games such as this help them to discover the difference between solids and liquids and to judge spaces and distances.

The brain is the body's control centre and information store all rolled into one. It controls, directly or indirectly, everything that happens in our bodies.

At birth, the brain is large compared with other parts of a baby's body. If you look at a newborn baby, the head often seems too big for the tiny body and stick-like legs. The brain is already a quarter of the weight of an adult brain. A baby's body is only a twentieth of its adult weight. The brain grows fast. By the time the baby is one year old, the brain is half its adult weight. By the age of seven, the brain is almost fully grown. From then on, growth slows down. The brain will have reached its full size by the time we are about 20 years old.

Learning to learn

From the moment of birth, babies build on the instincts with which they arrived. They start to learn from the mass of stimuli coming in through all their senses.

The cells that receive these stimuli are called **nerves**. We have nerve endings all over our bodies. They pick up many details about shape, size, colour, smell, taste or pain. The information travels along the nerves to the brain where it is then stored.

The brain can also send out instructions along the nerves. These instructions control every movement we make, whether we are picking up a cup to drink from or playing a piece of music on the violin. This web of brain and nerve cells is called the **nervous system**.

At birth, many of the connections between brain and nerve cells have not fully grown. In the first weeks and months, whole new pathways are built in the brain. As the nervous system grows and matures, so babies learn how to get control of the various parts of their bodies. Babies may first find out that they can move their own hands when they reach out for a rattle or toy. Later on they learn how to open and close their fingers to grip the toy.

▼ The picture on the left was painted by a 2 year old. The picture on the right was the work of a 4 year old. As we grow older we learn to observe and to record what we see. We learn to control the muscles which help us paint and draw.

Many babies go through a time when they seem to enjoy dropping things over the side of a cot or pram. This is because they have at last got control over the nerves and muscles of the hand. This allows them to let go of things exactly when they want to. It can be very annoying for their parents!

A busy life

During the first five years, babies and young children learn faster than at any other time in their lives. During the first year, they learn about themselves, the things around them, their parents and family. In the second and third years, speech and language develop. This means that more and more complex ideas and experiences can be stored away in the memory.

Humans take about twenty years to become adults. This is longer than most other animals. Throughout the years of childhood, we learn new things all the time. As we get older, we go on learning. However, we never learn as quickly and easily as in the first few years of life.

► Young children like to have a story read to them before they go to bed. They learn to recognize pictures in the book. When they go to school, they learn to read for themselves.

Growing bigger

We all started off as one tiny fertilized egg. How does that simple cell become a thinking, moving, fully-working human being? The answer is, by growing. Growth is rather like an enormous sum. Cells divide in half, over and over again. The numbers get very large indeed. In a full-grown adult there are millions and millions of cells.

However, the dividing cells are not all identical to each other. Different cells do different work. How do particular groups of cells know what they should become?

When the first cell division takes place, each new cell carries the complete instructions to make an entire new person. As further divisions take place, it seems that most of these instructions switch off. They leave just the special information that will start the new cell growing into bone, muscle or a big toe-nail.

Growing bones

The most obvious way we grow is by getting taller. At our second birthday we are about half our final adult height. Most girls reach their final height at about fifteen. Boys reach theirs at about eighteen.

For us to grow taller, the long bones in our arms and legs have to get longer. Although bones look hard, they are living parts of our bodies. Bone cells get larger and divide just like any other cells.

Soon after birth, the ends of the long bones harden. In the middle of the bones, there is an area called a **growth plate**. At each end of the growth plate, the cells divide. This pushes the two ends of the bone further apart, making it longer. The growth plates gradually get smaller and disappear completely between the ages of 20 and 24.

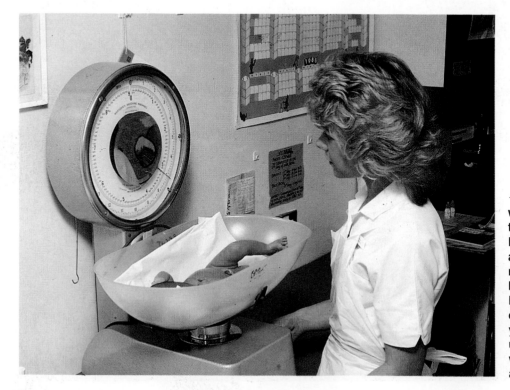

◄ In many countries, when babies are born they are weighed. Every few weeks they are weighed again to make sure that they keep on growing. Babies grow very quickly in the first year. They have usually doubled their weight before they are six months old.

▼ By the age of five years, many children have reached about two-thirds of their final height. We keep a record of children's height to make sure that they are developing normally.

How tall?

How short or tall we become depends on how fast we grow and for how long. This, in turn, depends on hormones. Growth hormone is made in the gland attached to the base of the brain, the **pituitary gland**. This growth hormone controls how fast we grow. Other hormones called **androgens** close the growth plates, so setting our final adult heights.

Exactly how tall we finally become depends to some degree on the body pattern passed on in our genes. It also depends on the kind of food and care we get as children.

Not getting enough food, or eating food without the right balance of nutrients in it, can cause problems. This **malnutrition** means that children may not be as healthy nor grow as tall as they otherwise would.

▼ Even when we are fully grown we will not all be the same height. These children are all the same age but some are much taller than others. The ones who are short now may not be the shortest when they are adults.

Off to school

During the first five years, our body systems grow and develop at a great rate. At three years old, a child still has the chubby legs and arms, and the large head of a baby. By five, the babyish look has gone. Instead, there is a slim, leggy child.

At five years old, the brain is 75 per cent of its adult weight. By six, it has reached 90 per cent of its adult weight, and the nerve fibres are almost complete. For the first two or three years, children learn to make sense of what they hear, see and feel. The people who are important to them are their parents, or whoever takes care of them, and any brothers and sisters. Two-year-olds like to be with other children but they often squabble with each other. They have not yet learned how to share and co-operate with others.

▲ As we grow we are able to do very intricate tasks, like doing up shoe buckles.

◀ At school, we do not simply learn facts and figures off by heart. We learn how to find things out for ourselves, and we learn very quickly. Only a few years before, these pupils would have been playing like the children on page 30. Now they can carry out scientific experiments.

Learning new skills

During the school years, children go on growing. They get stronger, and are able to move faster and more easily. They have already learned many basic skills from how to walk and talk to how to feed themselves and put on their clothes. The children have learned much of this simply by copying. Now the children can take in instructions. This helps them to learn a variety of new things, from tying their shoelaces to how to swim or cook biscuits. When a child reaches school age, children of the same age group, or **peers**, become important. Being accepted by our peers as part of the group is often more important even than fitting in at home.

Learning through play

'It's child's play', people say, to suggest that something is easy. However, child's play is more important than it looks. Playing with toys and with other children prepares children for the adult world.

Playing with a toy tea-set in a play house helps a five-year-old learn about size and shape. It is a way of copying skills from parents. Play also develops imagination with 'let's-pretend' games. It also teaches children how to solve problems.

Later, through the rough-and-tumble of playground games, children learn how to respond to their peers. They find out how to deal with other people and where to draw the line in a quarrel. Children also learn to tell the difference between right and wrong. It is all practice for the grown-up world when getting on with other people is no longer just a game.

▼ Dressing up as adults, and copying the things that adults do is an important part of growing up. These children are playing at 'weddings'. They have learned how to work together and to organize themselves, so they can each have a part to play.

Growing up

Compared with many animals, humans are quite old before they can reproduce. During the last years of childhood, many changes take place inside our bodies. All these changes are preparing us for the time when we will have children of our own. This time of change between childhood and adulthood is called **puberty**.

Growing and changing

Men and women have cells that come together to start a new baby growing. The biggest difference between the male and the female is that a new baby has to live and develop for nine months inside the female. Afterwards, the mother will go on feeding the baby with milk from her own body.

The changes needed to prepare both male and female bodies for all this are brought about by hormones. During childhood, the brain makes more and more of two special hormones. When these hormones have built up to a certain level, they cause other hormones to be released from the testes in boys and from the ovaries in girls. These hormones gradually spread all over the body.

In girls, the increase in hormone levels happens between about 10 and 12. It starts to bring about the body changes of puberty. The girl's breasts begin to develop. Hair begins to grow under her arms and between her legs. The most important sign of puberty comes when the first egg is released from the ovaries. The monthly cycle of menstruation has begun.

In boys, puberty is often a little later. Sperm begin to be made. The body gets more muscular and hair grows on his chest, under the arms and between his legs. Boys' voices 'break', or get deeper.

◀ As children reach puberty their bodies change. They become stronger and better at many sports, particularly swimming. This girl is building up her muscles for swimming in competitions.

▲ This thirteen-year-old Jewish boy is preparing for his bar mitzvah. The ceremony will mark his passing from boyhood and his growing up. Similar ceremonies are held in many parts of the world.

Getting together

For new life to be made, and for the human species to continue, couples must get together in the act of sexual intercourse. The changes that happen in puberty are all geared towards making reproduction possible. They also make the male and female more attractive to each other. This is the time when young people start getting interested in each other as boyfriends and girlfriends.

Some of the changes caused by hormones can be seen clearly. Other changes are not so obvious. During puberty, young adults still need their parents, but they must also make the first moves towards managing on their own. This is the time when they show this new **independence** in the clothes they wear, the hairstyles they choose, or in the interests they have.

▲ Teenagers like to develop in a way that is obviously different from their parents. This group of girls have formed their own rock group. They are not dressed as their mothers would be!

37

Adults and families

▼ When we are grown up, work may take up most of our time. We work in order to raise money to keep ourselves and our families. We take part in the society in which we live.

The growth spurt of puberty comes to an end at the age of about eighteen. At this stage in their lives, teenagers are growing away from their parents. The skills learned throughout childhood now prove very useful. They are needed because becoming independent usually means getting a job and setting up home.

Physically, a teenager of this age is ready to reproduce. That has been the purpose behind all the body's growth and development. Boys reach the peak of their reproductive lives between the ages of 20 and 24. This means that they are most capable of reproducing, or **fertile**. Girls are most fertile a little later, at about the age of 24. Of course, many people have children earlier and later than this.

Having a family

The human child needs years of care. It is usually the mother and the father who help and support him or her through this time.

Unlike most animals, human parents usually live together with their children. Two parents living together with their children is a common pattern of family life. They often live together in a larger group with other relatives. This is called an **extended family**. Sometimes the parents and children live alone together in a **nuclear family**.

These are not the only ways of bringing up children. Sometimes parents separate and bring up children alone. They may even remarry and so the family becomes extended. Sometimes a husband has several wives. Sometimes a wife has several husbands. In some parts of the world, the children in the community are looked after as a group.

Whatever the number of parents, stepparents or carers, a good family group will provide care, love and a stable background for the children.

The end of having children

Men can go on making sperm and fertilizing ova until old age. Women, however, cannot always produce ova. Once again, the change is brought about by hormones. Between the ages of about 40 and 50, there is a drop in the level of the hormone **oestrogen** in a woman's body. This slows down and eventually stops the release of ova from the ovaries. When a woman's menstrual periods stop completely, her child-bearing days are over.

▲ Much of our adult life is spent organizing the house and raising children.

▼ In some parts of the world, people do not live in small nuclear families. In this long-house in Borneo, the children of many different families are all brought up together.

Growing old

People are living longer than they used to. Thirty years ago, the average age all over the world was only about 47 years. By the end of this century, the average age is expected to go up to 64 years. As we get older, cells all over the body stop working so well.

Signs of old age

How soon we start to show the signs of old age varies from person to person. When hair goes grey it is an obvious sign of old age. This starts happening to many people in their forties, though it can be much earlier. There are cells in the skin which make a substance called **melanin**. Melanin gives hair its colour. When melanin is no longer made, the outer layer of the hair is colourless, so it looks grey.

▲ Hair usually keeps on growing until the end of our lives. However it often looses its colour after the age of thirty. The cells that make the hair colour stop working. The hair becomes grey and then white.

◀ Women generally live longer than men. These twins are well over 90 years old. Although their hair is white, their skin wrinkled and they need glasses, they still enjoy life.

40

Wrinkles are another clear sign of ageing. As we get older, the fibres in the skin get more stretchy. This means that the skin becomes less firm and falls into wrinkles. This happens all the more if skin is exposed to sunlight. Faces usually look more wrinkled than any other part of the body.

Inner signs

From the moment the brain is fully grown, it starts to age. Every day, from the age of about twenty, we loose 10 000 or so brain cells. This is still only a minute fraction of the total number we are left with in old age. As people get older, the brain does not work as well as it used to. For example, old people often find it hard to remember things that happened recently, while they can remember events from distant childhood very clearly.

Blood vessels, muscles and bone all suffer in the ageing process. Blood vessels often get narrower and the heart pumps the blood less easily. Muscles get smaller. As they are used less they get weaker. Bone, too, is lost. As we get less active, our bones get lighter and more brittle. They are more likely to snap under sudden pressure.

Getting old sounds a gloomy prospect. Yet many old people feel younger than they look. Many eighty-year-olds look far younger than they actually are. Staying active by taking exercise keeps muscles and bones strong.

When
people die

▼ At this Christian funeral in Switzerland, the dead body is placed inside a wooden coffin. Members of the dead man's family carry flowers in his memory. The coffin will be buried in the ground.

There are things we can do to slow down the ageing process. Exercise and the right kind of food help to avoid many of the diseases of old age. So far, however, no-one has found a way of stopping the slow crumbling of all the body's organs. In the end, death comes to us all.

What is death?

As we get older, the heart, lungs, kidney and liver work less and less well. To stay alive and healthy, our bodies rely on the heart to pump blood through a network of blood vessels. Blood carries the nutrients and oxygen we need to every cell in the body. In old age, the heart often cannot keep up with the demand for food and oxygen. It falters and stops. When the heart stops beating, blood stops flowing.

Cells all over the body are starved of food and oxygen. Different cells can last for a longer or shorter time. Brain cells can only survive for a matter of seconds without a blood supply.

A time for sadness

Most people want to go on living as long as they can. It is part of the natural drive to survive that is built into our genes. Yet it seems that we are programmed to die when we get old, just as we are programmed to survive as newborn babies. This programming allows for change and variety.

The death of a friend or a family member is usually a time of great sadness. Knowing that the dead person is lost forever is often very hard to accept.

▲ When a body is burned, it is called cremation. At this funeral in Bali, Indonesia, the dead body is cremated with elaborate ritual.

In memory

People all over the world have different ways of marking death. The body of the dead person is usually burned or buried in a ceremony called a **funeral**. In some countries, this is a time of sadness or **mourning**. In others, it is a time for a party to celebrate life and the living. The funeral gives family and friends a chance both to remember the dead and to say goodbye. It is worth remembering that the dead person may well live on in genes passed on to the following generations.

▲ These girls in the Philippines light candles at this service in memory of the dead.

43

What will the future bring?

People have lived on Earth for about five million years. We started off as simple ape-like creatures. We learned to use tools. We learned the advantages of living in groups to make the best of food supplies.

As generation followed generation, so genes mixed with genes. Our minds and bodies changed little by little. Gradually we grew less ape-like and taller. Our brains grew bigger. A clever hunter would have more chance of surviving when times were hard and food was in short supply. It follows that his genes had more chance of being passed on to the next generation, and with his genes his hunting skills. This process of change happening generation by generation is called **evolution**.

The peak of achievement?

Will our bodies and minds continue to change and evolve? Perhaps we have already reached the height of our strength and achievement. Today we live in a world full of machines that are there to help us. Most of us no longer need to use our bodies to escape from wild animals or to hunt for food. If we need to travel faster or see further, we can use a car or a telescope. If we have trouble breathing or hearing there are machines to help us with these too.

Test-tube babies

Sometimes people find it difficult to have babies. In the last ten years, it has become easier for men and women who have these problems to have babies. Sperm and ova can now be collected and deep-frozen. Later on the ovum can be fertilized and put back into the mother's uterus where it grows like any other normal baby. The mother no longer needs to be the person who makes the ovum. People can now offer their own sperm and ova to men and women who would not otherwise be able to have babies.

Scientists are now working on ways of separating X and Y-carrying sperm. This could mean that, in the future, we may be able to choose to have boys or girls.

Modern medicine

The first people did not have doctors or medicines. If they were hurt or fell ill, they had to rely chiefly on the body's own defence system to heal itself. It was the weakest members of the group who died in an attack or from disease. Today, we have strong drugs to overcome many diseases. More of us than ever live to a ripe old age. Even if we are not 100 per cent healthy, we can expect to survive in order to pass on our genes to the next generation. It is likely that a broader and broader mix of genes will be passed on to give shape to future generations of humans.

▼ In the future, people may be able to live in space. By that time we may have mixed our genes so widely that people will look more alike. We may also know how to slow up the ageing process.

45

Glossary

amniotic fluid: a watery liquid which surrounds an unborn baby. The fluid protects the baby

amniotic sac: the bag shape tissue which surrounds a baby while it grows inside the mother

androgen: a substance that helps bring about some of the changes in our bodies as we grow up. It also helps control how tall we grow

antibody: a substance made by your body which protects the body against illness

cartilage: a tough, rubbery material found in various parts of the body. Some cartilage hardens into bone as we grow up

cell: a very small part or unit of a living animal or plant. Most living things are made up of millions of cells

cervix: the narrow opening into the part of the body where an unborn baby grows. The cervix gets much larger when the baby is to be born

chromosome: a tiny thread-like structure found in every one of your cells. Chromosomes are found in pairs and carry the instructions for how every part of the body will grow

colostrum: milk that is made just after a baby is born. It is very rich in important foods and helps protect the new baby from illness

contraction: getting smaller or drawing together. When a baby is ready to be born, the mother's womb muscles draw together to push the baby out of her body

dilate: to become larger or wider

environment: the combination of people, places and things around us

evolution: the way living things have reached their present form by slow and gradual change. This has happened over thousands of generations

extended family: any family group which includes more than parents and children

fallopian tubes: the tubes inside a woman's body that lead from where the eggs are stored to the uterus where an egg can grow into a baby. Eggs travel along the fallopian tubes to the uterus

fertile: being able to make young

fertilization: the moment male and female cells join up and start to grow into a baby

foetus: the young of an animal in the womb or in the egg

fraternal twins: two babies which have grown from separate eggs in the same mother's womb at the same time

funeral: the ceremony that takes place when a person's dead body is burned or buried

gene: the tiny parts in each living cell which makes up the pattern for how every part of the body will grow

genetics: the study of how body patterns made by genes are passed on from one generation to the next

germ: a tiny living thing which causes disease. Germs can be seen only with a very strong microscope

gland: a part of the body which makes a substance for the body to use. Different glands make different substances

growth plate: a part of the bones where growth takes place. They gradually get smaller and disappear completely when the bones are fully grown

heredity: the way certain features of the parents are passed on to the following generations

hormone: a substance made in the body to trigger off changes, like growth. Hormones are carried around the body in the bloodstream

identical: exactly the same

identical twins: when two babies grow from the same fertilized egg. The babies have the same body pattern and so look exactly alike

independence: being able to survive without depending on others

instinct: behaviour which we carry out without thinking or learning about it

malnutrition: illness caused by having too little food, or by eating the wrong sort of food

melanin: a layer of dark colouring which is found in skin and hair

menstruation: when the thick lining or menses, of the womb is got rid of, together with a small amount of blood

midwife: someone who is trained to look after a mother while she is pregnant and at birth of the baby

mourning: feeling sadness at losing someone who has died

multiple birth: when a woman gives birth to more than one baby at a time

muscle: a type of material in the body which tightens and relaxes to produce movement

nerve: one of a network of tiny fibres which pass messages from all parts of the body and brain

nervous system: the interconnected network of nerves, brain and spinal cord

nuclear family: a family group made up of just the parents and children

nutrient: the part of any food which can be used by the body for health and growth

oestrogen: a substance in the body which makes the female become able to have babies

organ: a part of the body which has a particular job, such as the brain or stomach

ovary: one of the small structures in the female body where eggs are stored

ovum: a tiny part in the female body which can be fertilized and grow into a new member of the species

peer: a person in your age group who is similar to you

penis: the part of the male body which lets out waste water and is used to fertilize the female egg

pituitary gland: a small part of the body at the base of the brain. It makes several substances which help control functions of the body such as the rate of growth

placenta: the structure that grows inside the mother's body to pass on food and oxygen to the unborn baby from the mother

pregnant: when a female has a baby growing inside her. Different animals are pregnant for different lengths of time

puberty: the time between about 12 years and 18 years when the human body grows and develops from a child to an adult

reproduction: the way plants and animals make new versions of themselves

scrotum: the part of the male body that contains the cells used to make a female egg grow

semen: a liquid made in the male body to carry the tiny cells used to make a female egg grow

sex: one of either of two groups, the male or female, of any species

sexual intercourse: when a male and female come together in the act which may start a new baby growing

sexual reproduction: a way of making a new plant or animal by joining some parts of the male and female of the same plant or animal

short-sighted: only being able to see clearly for a short distance

skeleton: the framework of bones that supports the body of some animals

species: a group of animals or plants which look alike and can breed with one another

sperm: the tiny part of a male which joins up with the female egg to start a new baby growing. They are one of the smallest cells in the body

stimuli: things that trigger action or have an effect on whatever they fall upon

taste bud: a tiny part of the tongue which picks up different tastes. These are sweet, sour, bitter and salt

testis: one of two parts of a male body which makes the cells used to reproduce young

umbilical cord: the tube that joins the unborn baby to the mother. It carries food and oxygen from the mother's bloodstream to the baby

uterus: the part of a woman's body where an unborn baby grows. It is also called the womb

vagina: the part of a woman's body that goes from the womb to the outside world

vasa deferentia: one of the two tubes leading from the testes in the male body to the outside

Index